flowers
A to Z

A PRACTICAL GUIDE TO

Buying | Growing | Cutting | Arranging

by Cecelia Heffernan

Photography by T. K. Hill

Harry N. Abrams, Inc., Publishers

EDITOR: Margaret L. Kaplan

DESIGNER: Miko McGinty

Library of Congress Control Number:
2001134060
ISBN 0–8109–2122–7

Portions of this book were previously
published in *Flowers A to Z: Buying,
Growing, Cutting, Arranging*, copyright ©
2001 Cecelia Heffernan, published by
Harry N. Abrams, Incorporated, New York.

Published in 2002 by Harry N. Abrams,
Incorporated, New York

Printed and bound in Hong Kong
10 9 8 7 6 5 4 3 2

Harry N. Abrams, Inc.
100 Fifth Avenue
New York, N.Y. 10011
www.abramsbooks.com

Abrams is a subsidiary of

CONTENTS

HARDWARE

1. Floral shears are used for cutting most flower stems. The blades should be thin and very sharp, to make a clean cut. Do not use standard scissors to cut your flowers: They have thicker blades and will close the stem partway when cut, impairing the absorption of water.

2. Floral shears with long, thin blades are useful for trimming flowers and stems in bouquets, or cutting flowers from the garden in hard-to-reach places. These should be very sharp as well, to make a clean cut.

Phlox →

Cut or purchase when two-thirds of the florets are open and the closed buds show good size and color—those cut in the tight bud stage will not develop. Phlox are very easy to grow, but be sure to remove spent flower heads so that the seeds cannot create undesirable new plants that may crowd out the main plant. Phlox attract butterflies to the garden. See care and conditioning tip 24 and arranging tips 12, 13, and 14.

3. Floral pruning shears are used for cutting thick, fibrous stems, and for thin, woody stems such as azaleas, hydrangeas, etc. The blades should be sharp and able to penetrate the stem and make a clean cut.

4. Heavy-duty pruning shears are used to cut and split thick branches.

Camellia →

Camellias should be cut or bought when the buds show good size and color, and are starting to crack open. This will ensure that they develop and blossom fully. Camellia blossoms are lovely floated in a bowl of water, and the foliage can be used when arranging with most types of flowers. See arranging tips 6 and 16, and care and conditioning tips 5, 6, and 24.

5. A hammer is used to split woody stems and branches.

6. A stem stripper is used to clean leaves, thorns, and small branches from the main stem. Be careful not to strip and bruise the main stem, which would shorten the life of the flower by contaminating the water with debris.

7. A floral or paring knife is used to trim thorns, leaves, and small branching stems from the main stem. The knife can also be used to cut the end of stems at an angle.

←
Hypericum

(Hypericum Berries, St.-John's-Wort). Purchase or cut when the berries are large and full, with a smooth, firm appearance. The small, yellow blossoms are widely used as a natural treatment for depression and to promote well-being (check with your doctor). The berries are wonderful to use in arrangements, because they do not fall off the stem as most berries do when handled. See care and conditioning tips 5 and 6.

8. Pure, clean water is best for flowers. Some of the elements in tap water can be harmful for flowers—for example, too much fluoride or iron. A water purifier attached to your tap will help.

9. Mild soap and bleach are needed to clean flower containers thoroughly. A drop of bleach with mild soap cleans any residue and kills bacteria that might inhibit the life of flowers. Premix the bleach, soap, and water in a large spray bottle, and keep on hand.

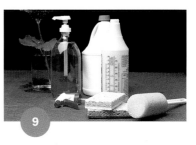

10. Twine and threads in shades of browns and greens are used for several purposes. See care and conditioning tips 17 and 29 and arranging tip 17.

←
Dahlia

Buy dahlias when they are three-fourths to fully open. Outer petals should not be discolored or wilted. Flowers will last longer if foliage and buds are removed; when they begin to wilt, gently pull off the outer petals for a fresh-looking smaller flower. See care and con-ditioning tips 25, 26; arranging tips 6 and 16; and growing tip 18.

11. A meat baster or a thin-spouted watering can is useful for keeping containers filled and stems in deep water. These choices make it easy to fill containers that hold several stems or branches.

12. Gloves keep hands protected from stains or the harmful secretions of certain flowers. Medical gloves work well, since they are thin and tight-fitting and don't interfere with the handling of the flowers.

13. A mister is used to cool flowers temporarily while providing an extra source of water and moisture.

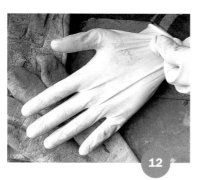

Euphorbia   →

(Spurge). There are more than 8,000 varieties. Purchase or cut when most of the flowers are open. The leaves often wilt after these flowers are cut, so remove them at the start. Euphorbias secrete a poisonous milky sap that may cause skin irritation and will cause illness if ingested. Wear gloves when handling them. See care and conditioning tip 27.

14. Floral wire is used for many purposes, such as repairing and straightening flowers. See care and conditioning tip 31 and arranging tips 18 and 20.

15. Floral tape and regular heavy-duty tape, such as duct tape, are useful. See care and conditioning tip 31e and arranging tip 19.

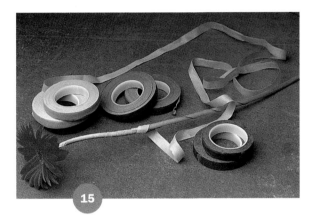

←
Snapdragon

A fresh snapdragon has a few blossoms open at the base of the flower spike, with the others in bud stage and showing good size and color. The flower is mostly upright. Cutting off the tightly budded tips encourages the other blooms to open sooner. However, the closed blossoms and green tips lend color and texture to an arrangement. If you gently squeeze the side of a snapdragon blossom, you will see how the flower gets its name, for the blossoms resemble the mouth of a dragon. See care and conditioning tips 8, 24, 32, 34, 35; arranging tips 12, 13, 15, 16; and growing tip 17.

16. An assortment of plastic or glass containers in various sizes is needed for proper hydration of the flowers.

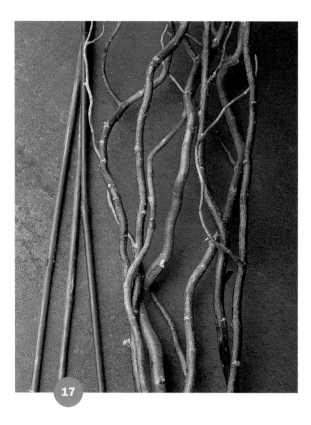

17. Straight branches or sticks such as bamboo or willow branches aid in supporting heavy flowers for proper hydration. See care and conditioning tip 29 and arranging tip 17.

18. Heavy paper, such as newspaper or butcher's paper, aids in straightening and supporting certain flowers. See care and conditioning tip 35.

Chrysanthemum →

There are about 1,000 varieties, including the common daisy. Mums are best purchased or cut when the flowers are fully open, show good color, and are firm to the touch. Because chrysanthemums give off large amounts of gas and bacteria, their thick, coarse stems should simply be cut on the diagonal rather than being hammered or split. Be sure to change the water frequently. Since mums can shorten the life of other flowers, they are best used alone. See also care and conditioning tips 13 and 26.

1. Do not place flowers directly into containers that are metal, rusted, or made of clay or stone. These materials are porous, and may contain elements that are harmful to flowers. It is best to line your container with glass or plastic. Glass and plastic are the best materials to contain flowers.

2. Containers should be clean and sterile before being filled with water and flowers. Clean, sterile containers are essential to the vase life of the flowers.

←
Calla lily

(Arum lily, Zantedeschia). A fresh calla is mostly open, but with the outer petals still reaching upward. The middle of the flower is clean, with no signs of pollen. The flower shows good color with no bruising. Callas have a long vase life owing to their thick, spongelike stems, but be sure to recut stems every few days to maintain a steady flow to the blossoms. See also care and conditioning tip 35.

3. Containers should be as deep as possible, considering the length of the flower stem. Flowers last longer in deep water.

Viburnum   →

(Snowball). Purchase or cut when the flower clusters are rather more green than white, the florets tight together, the cluster compact. In fall and winter, they produce attractive berries and fruit. Viburnum can be cut down and the blossoms used much like hydrangeas. See care and conditioning tips 5, 6, 26, 32 and arranging tips 8, 12, 13, and 14.

HANDLING FLOWERS

1. Always cut stems at a sharp angle. This increases the surface area of the stem and allows water to be better absorbed through the stem.

2. Stems cut at an angle will not rest flush against the bottom of the container; thus they allow the water to penetrate the stem.

3. After the end of the stem is cut, place it directly into the water. It only takes a minute for the stem to begin to dry and seal up.

4. Thick stems and thin branches should be cut at an angle, and then cut up the center for better water absorption through the fibrous stems.

5. Hammer all thick, woody stems and branches about five to six inches up from the bottom, and make several splits in the stem. This allows for better water absorption.

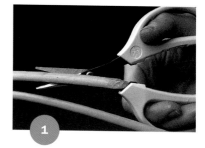

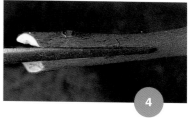

Bouvardia →

Buy bouvardia when it is mostly in bud stage, with only one or two flowers open. The buds should show good color. Their size is important, since bouvardia is often cut prematurely in the flower trade. To prolong vase life, frequently recut the stems and place in deep, fresh warm water. Tear off excess greenery and blossoms so that more water reaches the primary blooms. See care and conditioning tips 4, 24, and 32.

6. Remove the extra bark around the shattered part of the stem to prevent contaminating the water. This will prolong the vase life of the flowers.

7. Scrape off all the small debris on the stem—such as small thorns, branching stems, etc.—with a sharp, curved knife to thoroughly clean the stem before it is placed in the water.

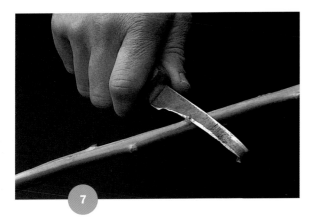

8. Pull or trim all leaves and thorns that will be below the water level in the container. Allowing such materials to decompose in water will allow harmful bacteria to shorten the life of the flowers.

←
Flowering quince

Flowering branches are best cut or purchased when the buds show good size and color, but even those in tight bud will fully develop in time. They are abundant in spring, but can easily be forced by bringing them indoors in February and March, after they have had a sufficient cold period. See care and conditioning tips 5, 6, 20, 24, 27, and arranging tip 9.

9. Clean stems should be placed in the deepest water possible to promote vase life. Water can be absorbed from the outside part of the stem as well as the base. A nick or crack in the stem left exposed above the water level can create an air pocket and block water flow to the flower. The deeper the water, the less likely this is to occur.

10. In conditioning flowers, the water temperature should be comfortably warm. Submerge your hand to test the water. Cold water is not as readily absorbed by the flower. Hot water will penetrate the stem, but will almost shock the flower.

11. Once flowers are placed in water, they begin to decompose or break down by releasing gases and forming bacteria. The cleaner the stems and the less debris in the water, the less decomposition occurs, and the longer the flowers will last.

Ranunculus   →

(French or Persian buttercup). Purchase or cut when the petals cup the middle of the flower and still fold inward. The flower should be firm and not shed when handled. Ranunculus are heavy drinkers, so watch the water level. Their stems break easily, making arranging tricky. See care and conditioning tips 31, 32, 34, and 35 and arranging tips 12, 13, 16, 17, 18, 19.

12. All the same kind of flower in a vase or container will last longer than a mix of different types. Certain flowers have a different makeup and decompose by different means. This mixed reaction can shorten the life of all the flowers. The same kind of flower will break down by the same reaction. Actually, a single flower in a vase will last even longer than several of the same kind.

Hyacinth   →

A fresh hyacinth has most of its flowers closed, with only a few opening at the base. The color is strong, the scent sweet. The thick, white, fibrous base should be cut off, to let water penetrate the stem. A single bulb forced in a glass is the perfect way to appreciate this flower. Note: hyacinths are poisonous—see care and conditioning tip 28; also growing tips 10, 11, and 12.

13. Cloudy or discolored water is an indication of decomposition and bacterial growth. Change the water in the container at least every couple of days, using new, warm water. This will open the stems to allow water to flow to the flower.

14. Fresh, clean water is best for the vase life of flowers. Some commercial floral foods can lengthen the vase life as well, but be very careful in measuring the amount. Using too much can actually be harmful. Homemade versions or substitutions, such as lemon lime soda, are not a good idea, because sugar promotes bacterial growth in the water.

15. Stems will develop a film and become discolored from stagnating in the water; this blocks water flow to the flower. Recut the stems each time the water is changed to allow water to penetrate the stem.

16. Mixed arrangements are sometimes hard to disassemble to change the water and to recut the stems. Flushing the container with fresh water will help somewhat to prolong the life of the bouquet. Use the tap or the spray nozzle on your sink full force for a few minutes to flush the container completely with warm water.

Yarrow   →

(Achillea). Purchase or cut when the flowers within the clusters are close together and upright. Most of the flowers should be open or just starting to open. If cut in bud stage, they will not open. Yarrows can easily wilt after cutting, so condition flowers and foliage in deep water for several hours. Yarrows will last longer as a shorter flower, so cut them down and use them as the base for arrangements. See care and conditioning tips 32, 34 and arranging tips 12 and 13.

17a, b, c. Use a piece of heavy twine to tie your arrangement at the top of the container. Once the flowers are tied snugly, pull them from the vase. Clean the vase, and change the water. Hold the tied bouquet upside down. Recut all the stems at an angle. Place back into the container and cut the twine. Your bouquet should fall back into place.

←
Bells of Ireland

(Moluccella, Shellflower). The shell petals of fresh bells of Ireland are open and the small white flowers are exposed. The spikes are straight and firm to the touch. As the flower ages, the tips begin to droop and the spike becomes soft to the touch. See care and conditioning tips 24 and 35.

18a, b. Many flowers will open in the light. This does not mean they are not fresh. It is the nature of that type of flower, which will close again in the dark. Temperature will also cause the same effect. Warmer temperatures will cause the flower to open, and cooler temperatures will cause it to close.

19. Flowers last best in temperatures around 45 degrees. Misting flowers with cold water a few times a day will cool them and create this environment temporarily. Flowers can also absorb this extra moisture through their petals.

←
Anemone

(Windflower). A fresh anemone has a tight, clean center without pollen developing. The petals show good color and are close together, forming a cup shape. Keep anemones in medium light and in a cool spot to prolong vase life. Also, anemones are heavy drinkers, so check the water level daily. See care and conditioning tips 18 and 35.

20. Keep flowers out of direct light. Flowers will last longer in a place of low to indirect light. Light creates heat and speeds up the life cycle of the flower. However, flowers with a green tinge owing to early cutting, or tightly budded flowers and branches, will need a strong light source to develop. Once the flowers show full color, put them in a place with less light so they will last.

21. Most flowers are accustomed to the outdoors, so air circulation is important for their vase life. Keep them in a place with good airflow. Cigarette smoke is harmful to flowers.

22. Many believe that placing flowers in the refrigerator at night helps them last longer. However, many foods may cause a negative reaction in the flowers from the gases they release in the breakdown process. Placing your flowers next to a window or in a cool room at night is a good idea.

Lilac →

(Syringa). Cut or purchase when most of the blossoms are open. Those cut in the tight-bud stage probably will not open. Cut lilacs last only a few days, but respond to very warm water changed frequently. Though lovely in mixed bouquets, they last longer when used alone. See care and conditioning tips 5, 6, 32, and arranging tips 8 and 14.

23 (photo number)

23. Purchased cut flowers will usually be wrapped in paper or cellophane to protect them. It is a good idea to leave them wrapped and hydrating in deep water for about an hour when they are brought home before conditioning or arranging them. This will ensure the flowers will be upright.

24. Pinching or trimming off spent blossoms and leaves encourages other blossoms to open and makes the flower last longer. The spent blossoms take some of the energy the flower needs to stay alive. Trimming these away allows the flower to channel the energy to the healthy parts.

24 (photo number)

←
Geranium

(Pelargonium). Fresh geraniums have a few flowers opening on the cluster, with more buds showing good color. They add intense color to summer bouquets, and the foliage of the scented varieties (lemon, rose, nutmeg, even chocolate) can be substituted for that of flowers that have no fragrance. See care and conditioning tip 24 and arranging tip 16.

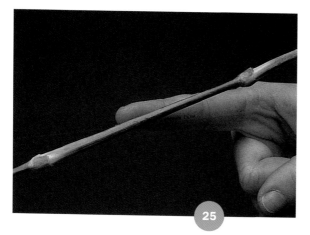

25. Some flowers, such as carnations and dahlias, have separations or nodes along their stems. The stem is thicker and more fibrous at these parts. Cut the stem between the nodes to allow water to penetrate the stem.

26. Branching or spray flowers will last longer if the stems are separated at their base. This allows for water to be directly absorbed by each blossom.

Carnation →

(Dianthus). Buy carnations when they are half open, and the miniature spray variety when it has a few flowers half to fully open, with the others in bud. The large blooms can be cut down and massed together in a tight bunch, so that they almost resemble garden roses or peonies. See also arranging tip 12 and care and conditioning tips 25 and 26.

27a, b. Some flowers secrete sap or latex when cut. Singeing the ends will keep this fluid contained in the stem. The fluid is what the flower needs to last. Some believe that placing the end in boiling water will seal the stem. This works, but the hot steam is not good for the flower itself; burning the end works the best. Try using a gas flame on a stove, or a candle with an extra-thick wick. Singe about one-half to one inch of the base of the stem.

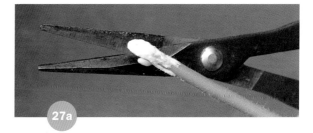

28. Poisonous flowers are best used alone in their own container. These flowers secrete latex that is harmful to other flowers. Condition by standing them in deep water with a drop of bleach for 24 hours before mixing with other flowers.

←
Daffodil

(Narcissus is the formal name). Cut or purchase when in the bud stage. The spray varieties may have one or two blooms opening. When picking, pinch the stems at the base with your fingers to partially close the stem. This will inhibit the latex serum from contaminating the water. Daffodils are best used alone unless properly conditioned. See care and conditioning tip 28 and growing tips 10, 11, and 12.

29. Tall or heavy flowers, such as lilies and hybrid delphiniums, may bend or break before they are completely hydrated. Tie the tip of the flower and the middle part of the stem loosely with twine to a branch or stick to support the flower for proper hydration.

30a. Flowers with hollow stems, such as amaryllis, are designed to draw water up through the outer layers of the stem. Some believe that filling the stem with water and plugging the end will help the flower last longer. This may help, but it is unnecessary because of the way the flower is designed.

30b. Hollow stems will crack and break more easily than solid stems. Support them by slowly inserting a stick into the end of the flower. A clean branch or bamboo works well. Covering the stick with a soft, water-absorbent material will protect the inside of the stem and provide extra moisture as well.

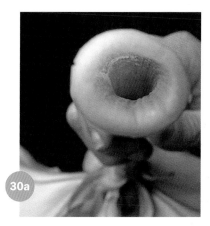

←
Delphinium

A fresh flower has three-fourths of its blossoms open, with only a few buds on the tip of the stem. Stalks in total bud will not open. The petals will not shed when handled. Note that some varieties are extremely poisonous. Delphiniums are heavy drinkers and feeders. See care and conditioning tips 8, 24, 29, 30, 31; arranging tips 13, 15, 16; and growing tip 18.

31a. Bent or cracked stems and flowers that bend owing to their heavy heads can be salvaged with floral wire. Insert the wire partway into the strong area above the bend or break, or under the flower head. Also see arranging tip 18.

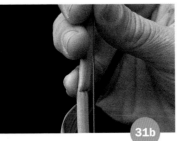

31b. Support the stem with the wire and straighten it to the upright position.

31c. Gently wrap the wire around the rest of the stem.

31d. Wrap the stem or the point of incision with floral tape to keep air from blocking water to the stem.

←
Lily

(Lilium). Purchase or cut when the bottom flower is just opening and the next two or three buds are full and show good color. Check for damage or discoloration on the closed blossoms. Lilies do not like flower preservatives or additives. Be careful not to crowd them in arrangements, since their large blossoms need room to open. See care and conditioning tips 24, 29, 31; arranging tips 8, 13, 14, 15, 16; and growing tip 12.

32. If flowers wilt or droop prematurely, cutting them short and placing them in slightly warmer water should revive them. Both the cutting and water temperature help the blossom absorb water more quickly.

33. Some flowers bend or droop because their flower heads become too heavy for their stems. The stems become waterlogged and stop conveying water to the blossom. A tiny prick just below the head of the flower will release air, thus increasing the water flow.

Sunflower   →

(Helianthus). Purchase or cut when three-quarters to fully open, with firm, slightly upturned petals. A clean center disk should show no signs of pollination and the flower should be sturdy and upright. When the petals fade, remove them and use the large disks for interesting texture in arrangements. See care and conditioning tips 4, 8, 29, 32; arranging tips 8, 14, 17; and growing tip 20.

34. Wilted flowers can also be revived by completely submerging them in cool water. Do this by filling a deep bucket or tub with cool water. Place the flowers lying down in the water and weigh them down with a weight of some kind, like a brick. Let the flowers stay submerged for a few hours.

Rose →

(Rosa). Buy or cut roses when a few outer petals are opening and the swirl of petals in the middle is closed. The blossom should be a bit firm to the touch, with the feeling of several layers of petals to open. Roses that are very firm, with the petals curved inward with no signs of opening, are cut too early and will usually result in drooping heads. Spray fully open roses with "Crown and Glory," available at florists, for a fresh, dewy appearance that holds at this stage for a couple of days. See care and conditioning tips 4, 7, 8, 26, 31, 32, 34 and arranging tips 8, 11, 13, 18, and 19.

35a. Some flowers bend or droop owing to light, temperature changes, or just because it is the nature of that flower.

35b. To straighten flowers, place them one by one on a damp paper, lining them up evenly.

35c. Gently roll the paper around the flowers, forming a cone shape.

35d. Secure the paper with twine or with staples so that the paper braces the flowers.

35e. Mist the flowers and paper to keep them damp. Place the cone of flowers in deep water for several hours.

35f. Unwrap the flowers and they will be upright again.

35d

35e

35f

1. The best way to arrange flowers is to approximate their natural state. If the flower is tall, opens, leans, etc., arrange it to suit that characteristic. Even if the flower is manipulated somewhat to fit into a certain type of arrangement, it is still best to utilize it according to its character. Let vines drape around the base of arrangements, leave room for flowers to open and close, etc.

2. Floral foam is very useful in flower arranging, because it holds each flower in place. However, when stems are inserted into foam, the foam covers and clogs the ends. The flowers will not last as long as when they are arranged in water.

3. The best way to start an arrangement is by making a good base. Many believe in using arranging devices such as floral foam, frogs, chicken wire, etc. These items are quite useful, but may create an almost unnatural bouquet as well as shortening the vase life of the flowers.

4. Arranging frogs have a similar effect on flowers. The end of the stem is partially blocked by the prongs inserted into the stem, inhibiting water flow to the flower.

5a. Chicken wire wedged into the container adds a metal material to the water that may react with the flowers. It can also damage stems as they are being placed into the container, thus further contaminating the water.

5b. Chicken wire secured around the top of the container is a better method.

6. A more natural way of starting an arrangement is to create a base with full, thick foliage. This base will help secure flowers in place when building an arrangement. Pick foliage that is similar to the flower choices for the most natural look.

7. When creating a base for an arrangement with foliage or flowers, place a few stems into the container and turn the container. Repeat this a few times to create a maze of intertwining stems. This will hold the other flowers and material in place to build the arrangement.

8. When flowers are cut shorter to use in bouquets, the best "filler," or greenery, is the flowers' own foliage. Save the excess that is cut off for use in and around the flowers.

Zinnia   →

Buy or cut when three-fourths to fully open. Cut too early, they will wilt prematurely. The petals should be of good color and the flower upright and firm. The middles should be clean, with little pollen formation. Zinnias have hollow stems that bruise, bend, and break easily, so handle with care. When growing zinnias in the garden, be careful not to get too much water on blossoms or foliage, since they are prone to mildew. See arranging tips 18 and 19.

9. When arranging in a vase that is too large for the number of flowers being used, fill the vase with the base of a branch. The branch acts as a natural maze for the flowers to brace against. The flowers stay in place as you build the arrangement, enabling you to use fewer of them.

10. Flowers with large, curved leaves, such as tulips, can be useful in arranging because the leaf left intact can act as a brace for the flower, and a few can make a nice base for other flowers to be added.

11. Leaving the thorns on stems is another way to create a natural base for a flower arrangement. The thorns will hold the stems together, so other flowers added will also be held in place.

←
Sweet pea

(*Lathyrus odoratus*). Purchase or cut when only a few of the bottom blossoms are fully open and some large, closed buds are ready to bloom at the top. Flowers will last longer if the stems are trimmed away from the central vine. Also, the more flowers you cut, the more new blossoms will be produced. Soaking sweet pea seeds overnight before planting will help them sprout sooner. Note that sweet pea seeds and flowers are poisonous. See care and conditioning tips 24, 26; arranging tips 1, 8, 12; and growing tip 20.

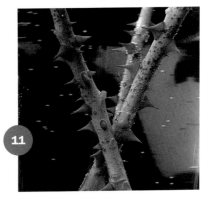

12. Tying a grouping of flowers like snapdragons or carnations together with thread or twine can create a nice base for arrangements. This method can also be used in securing taller stems of the same type of flower when building an arrangement. This is much easier than securing individual stems.

13. Tall flowers can be cut short and short flowers can be lengthened to suit the arrangement. See arranging tip 20.

14. Use large-blossomed flowers such as hydrangeas or amaryllis cut down for the base of an arrangement. The blossoms fill the vase opening, allowing the other flowers to be secured among and around them.

Stock   →

Fresh stock has one-third to one-half of its blossoms open, with the rest showing good color and size. The stem is very dense, making water penetration difficult and shortening vase life. If the thick, white, fibrous base remains, cut it away. Change the water and recut the ends frequently. See care and conditioning tips 4, 8, 24, 32 and arranging tips 12, 13, 14, and 15.

15

15. Tall flowers with several graduating blossoms, such as gladiolus and snapdragons, can be cut at the tips to encourage the other blossoms to open more quickly. This does alter the natural appearance of the flower, but it is helpful in speeding the blooming process.

16. Some flowers continue to grow and develop in water after they are cut. These flowers are sometimes difficult to arrange, because they change daily. Use thin green thread or twine to tie them to a branch or sturdy flower in the arrangement, which helps keep them in place and tidy.

17. Tightly budded flowers can be added to arrangements for interesting texture and a natural look. Place them among the fully blossomed flowers.

16

17

Gladiolus   →

(Sword Lily). A fresh gladiolus has one or two open flowers at the base. These show no signs of drying at the edges. The next five or six buds show good color, and the tip is tightly budded (it usually does not develop after cutting). When buying, check the bloom count to make sure the lower blooms have not been pinched away. See arranging tip 15 and care and conditioning tips 24 and 29.

18a. Floral wires are useful in securing flowers or bending a flower a certain way to make it fit better into an arrangement. Place the wire just under the head. Insert the wire about one-eighth to one-quarter inch into the flower.

18b. Straighten the flower to an upright position, or bend the flower into the desired position.

18c. Gently fold the wire closely around the bottom part of the stem. The stem is now secured or can be maneuvered.

19. Wrapping floral tape similar in color to the stem around the length of the stem will hide the wire and aid in preventing an air pocket. See care and conditioning tip 31e.

20a. Floral wires are useful in lengthening the stems of flowers with short stems, or flowers that have been cut too short for an arrangement. Simply place the wire in the bottom of the stem about two inches, and cut the wire the desired length.

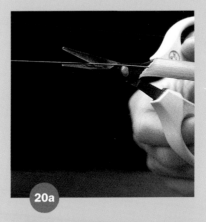

20b. The wire end will act as the stem end resting in the container.

21. There is a "rule" that an arrangement should be one and one-half times the height of the container. However, this rule does not necessarily apply. Flower stems submerged in a vase with just their heads peeking over the rim can be just as attractive as a proportioned bouquet.

22. The most elaborate combination or the simplest of bouquets can be transformed by the container choice. Pick a container to enhance the flowers. This bright yellow container displays the flowers in a more interesting way than would a plain glass vase.

Orchid →

When buying cut orchids, look for flowers that are open or beginning to open—tight buds probably will not bloom. Orchids love humidity, so frequent misting with lukewarm water will help prolong vase life. When growing as houseplants, make sure the roots are exposed, for humidifying and ventilation. Drench the roots and drain completely once a week. Mist often. See care and conditioning tips 24, 29, 34 and growing tips 4 and 5.

1. When planting, start with a good soil mix. Make sure it is light and airy, and rich in nutrients. If the soil is clayey or heavy, it may retain too much moisture or suffocate the plant. This is true whether you are planting in containers, forcing bulbs, or preparing your garden beds.

2. Most flowering plants and bulbs need proper watering to thrive. Too much water or too little can be harmful. Discoloration of leaves is an indication of a watering problem. If you can squeeze water from a handful of soil, then the plant has too much water. Water your plants gently, allowing them to drink slowly and being careful not to drench them all at once, which may give them a shock.

3. Some plants and bulbs prefer to be watered from beneath, so that they can absorb the amount they need slowly and hydrate as they wish.

←
Cyclamen

Plants should have only a few flowers fully open, with several in bud stage and more sprouting at the base. Spent flowers and yellow leaves should be removed promptly by trimming them away at the base of the stems. Water sparingly from beneath, to keep the roots from rotting. Keep in bright but indirect light in a cool spot. See growing tips 2, 3, 4 and care and conditioning tip 24.

4. Be careful not to leave container plants sitting in stagnant water that drains from a watering. Stagnant water causes plants to become too moist. Placing a few rocks or pebbles in the saucer allows excess water to drain.

5. Most flowering plants benefit from misting with cool water. The cooler temperature aids exterior water absorption and refreshes the plant.

Lily of the Valley →

(Convallaria). Cut or purchase when most of the blossoms are open, with just a few buds on top. The fragrance should be pleasingly strong. Lilies of the valley prefer a shady spot in the garden. The plants will take a few years to establish and flower, but then they will bloom spring after spring. See growing tips 10, 11, 12 and care and conditioning tip 34.

6. Water plants and flowers in the garden when the sun is low, either morning or evening. Do not water them in the heat of the day, when water on the flowers and leaves may scorch the plant.

7. Proper fertilization is helpful. Nutrients are important to a plant's development, but be careful not to overfertilize: More is not always better. Read instructions carefully and follow the guidelines. Too much fertilizer actually harms plants, inhibiting instead of promoting growth.

8. Cut flowers in the morning or evening. Flowers cut at midday may not hold up.

Iris   →

(Fleur-de-Lis). Iris should be cut or purchased in total bud stage. The flower opens quickly and lasts only a few days. The bud should be of good size and color and feel firm to the touch. If the tip is discolored or dry, the flower will not open. The miniature variety *Iris reticulata* can be forced to bloom indoors in winter. See arranging tip 13 and growing tips 10, 22, 12, and 19.

9. Flowers from the garden are the best source for cutting. However, when your garden is not producing in abundance, buy plants from nurseries, greenhouses, florists, and grocery stores. The flowers are still growing and can be kept until they are used. Cut what you need to use and allow the plant to produce more flowers.

9

10a. When forcing bulbs to bloom in winter, plant them shoulder to shoulder and leave the top one-third to one-half of the bulb exposed to prevent rot. Close planting and partial exposure cut down on excess moisture and allow a greater show of flowers.

10b. Gently scrape away the dry roots on the bottom of the bulb. It will root more quickly and be less likely to rot.

10a

←
Hydrangea

Fresh hydrangeas have most of the flowers in the cluster open. They can wilt easily once cut, so when conditioning the stems, drape cold, wet cloths over the blossoms and mist frequently for about four hours. Dip the bottom inch of the stems in boiling water and then in powdered alum (available at most grocers). See care and conditioning tips 4, 25, 26, 32 and arranging tip 14.

10b

11a. Place rocks or broken terra-cotta pieces in the bottom of the container before planting to help with drainage.

11b. Mixing a little sand and horticultural charcoal into the soil mixture also helps drainage and keeps the soil fresh.

12. When planting bulbs outside, they should generally be planted at a depth of two and one-half times their diameter. Bulbs planted too deep or too shallow will not perform as well.

13. Make sure bulbs and plants are not crowded when planted—the roots need room to grow if the plant is to flourish.

Amaryllis   →

(Hippeastrum, *Amaryllis bella-donna*, Belladonna Lily). A fresh amaryllis has its blossoms closed, or just one beginning to open. The buds show good color and size, and the stem feels strong and sturdy. Amaryllis in bud stage opens slowly and turns toward the light. Make sure the plant is in an evenly lit place, or turn it to ensure a well-developed blossom. See care and conditioning tip 30.

14. Cutting back garden plants after their flowering period or to produce more flowers should follow one rule: Only cut back what is dry and discolored. While a plant is green, it is still in its cycle, and cutting back too soon can actually inhibit growth for the next year.

15. Multiflowering plants should be trimmed back as the blossoms are spent to encourage more blooms to develop.

16. Some plants, such as delphinium, can be fooled into blooming a second time. Once a flower has bloomed, cut the entire plant back to the ground, leaving only the base of foliage. The plant will actually force itself to produce a second flower. It may lack some of the height and bloom count of the first, but for the most part will produce a second beautiful flower.

17. Some plants can be forced to become larger. When the plant sends up its initial flower stalk, cut the stalk back to the base of the leaves. The plant will then send up multiple shoots, producing more flowers.

←
Cosmos

Purchase cosmos when the flowers have just started to open but the petals are not completely lying flat. The buds will also open after the flowers are cut. Cosmos seeds can be sown directly into the soil after the danger of frost is over, and the blossoms will attract butterflies to the garden. See also care and conditioning tips 24 and 26.

18. To produce a large flower from a plant that usually produces several blossoms, focus on one bud, trimming the others away so the plant can focus its energy. This method is known as "disbudding."

19. Plants should be divided every few years to give them a vigorous new start and make them stronger bloomers. Wash away the soil from the roots before you make the division, so that you can see the best place to cut or pull. Be sure to leave a good clump of roots for each section.

20. When growing plants from seeds, make sure not to crowd them, as this will inhibit growth. If seedlings appear crowded, pull the smallest and weakest, concentrating on the healthy ones.

21. Protect your garden with nutrient-rich mulch over the winter, concentrating on the most frost-sensitive plants that need extra protection to survive. Plant according to your temperature zone if you want plants to return and thrive every year. Some perennials can be planted as annuals in cooler climates.

←
Agapanthus

(African Lily, Lily of the Nile). A fresh agapanthus has one-third of its blossoms opening, with the rest in bud stage. If you shake the flower gently, the blossoms will not fall off. When the flowers drop, cut back the small bare stems at the base of the cluster—this will help the other blossoms open. Agapanthus are tall, magnificent flowers, but can also be cut short and tucked into arrangements.